P9-AFE-016

THE GHOSTS OF WHO WE WERE

WITHDRAWN
UTSA Libraries

Poems by
Phyllis H. Thompson

THE
GHOSTS
OF
WHO
WE
WERE

University of Illinois Press
Urbana and Chicago

Publication of this work was made possible by a grant
from the National Endowment for the Arts.

© 1986 by the Board of Trustees of the University of Illinois
Manufactured in the United States of America

This book is printed on acid-free paper.

Acknowledgments: Abiding gratitude to the Corporation of Yaddo
for the right kind of place and time to write some of these poems.
Thanks also to the editors of the following periodicals in which
some of these poems appeared.
Hawaii Review: "Koetsu: Moon and Rabbit"; "Sunset"; "The City
   Is an Island"; "Kailua Beach"
The Paper: "Nausicaa"; "Rodolpho: A Later Winter"; "No One"
Prairie Schooner: "Home"; "Alone at Ainahou"; "December Light"
Three Rivers Journal: "What We Learned"
Hanai: "By Whose Authority?"
Wildflower: "Blue Flowers"
Graham House Review: "Blue Ginger: Déjà Vu"; "Letter from
   South of Rome"
Tarasque: "What Passed"; "Four Fishing Songs"
Choice: "Chartres"
New Letters: "The Chill of Distance"
Hudson Review: "The Ghosts of Who We Were"
Tendril: "On the Ledge"
New England Review: "A Gust of Winter"
Ironwood: "Hermione"; "At Ninety-Two"
Woman Poet I: "Rainwater"

Library of Congress Cataloging-in-Publication Data

Thompson, Phyllis H.
   The ghosts of who we were.

   I. Title.
PS3570.H643G5   1986   811'.54   85-20830
ISBN 0-252-01292-5

LIBRARY
The University of Texas
at San Antonio

For Mead, Willie, John, Kate
who deserved more mother than they got
I have one daughter and three sons
whose lives are my solace.
Their kindnesses scatter around me.

CONTENTS

I

The shade of our lost lives burns into bloom
And returns to us, trembling with imminence. . . .

KOETSU: MOON AND RABBIT

A March night, a cold moon
Where, in the moon's mortar,
The rabbit grinds the elixir of life.
But spring is too sweet, and he bounds
Down to the fragrant clover.

For months the moon has come and gone.
Gold. Now it hangs full,
Gorged with the ancient witness, heavy with travel.
All that time.
Now it is close to Earth.

The rabbit halts.
He looks back at the lowered moon
From the meadow he quivers in. The moon-colored clover
He nibbles is young as the spring grass
Against his soft pelt—that young.

Everything around him is
That young, except the moon's mortar and pestle
Hanging close enough to show him how long he's had to be quick.
There is no medicine for this appearance.
Tonight he will jump back into the moon.

for Darryl and Martin, remembering an "Exquisite Vision"

Dusk seems slow, the drifts of cirrus high.
My eyes still hurt from a sunny haze on the Bay
When the yachts headed out this morning. Gone all day.
Now in the gradually lavender sky
Stars are beginning. So many kinds of light.
I wonder how long I've been in this chair?
At least I'm not hungry. The air
Gets chilly near the ocean though, toward night.

"Warm enough?" My daughter. Voice like mine.
"I've brought you a sweater, Mother. Here. Soon
As I'm through I'll join you, to watch the moon
Come up." Beyond the purple line
Of spruce it will ride out, opalescent, white,
Huge over Newport, as it always does,
Then blue, till nothing is as it was—
The world undisturbed but utterly changed by moonlight.

Like that time at Gibson Island. Blossoming pear.
Full moon. A fragrance touched me. He touched. Who?
Softer than breath. Shivering petals flew
Where I stepped, shaken in windless air,
The night on fire with sweetness. When I tried
To speak, I couldn't . . . tears came. Youth.
I can't speak now. Words in my mouth
Get broken. All I feel is caught inside.

"I'm here now, Mother. I hate staying in
When the moon's rising. Near the wharf—look there."
The changing moon. What can I do but stare,
A dumb animal, at my close kin?
Half in another world and half in this,
Stricken, and from myself estranged.
In a twinkling we shall all be changed.
Possibly. Death is anybody's guess.

What will become of me? Maybe the soul, set free,
Scatters and clusters the way blue moonbeams break
To the ruffling Narragansett as a wake
Of pear petals. Moon blossoming sea.
The vision blurs. Too dark and bright. It's cold.
Light washes. Nothing. Null. The deep.
The years that empty into sleep.
It's damp out. Time to be taken in. I'm old.

for Eleanor, my sister

A CHILDHOOD

First snow had fallen.
Inside, cross-legged on the bare wood floor,
We faced one another.
Wrapped in warm blankets,
We talked all night.
There was no lamp. The moon
Filled the window and flooded the cold room
Moving slowly around the walls
And away by daybreak.

In half a century
I have been equally happy maybe five times.

You turned twelve in December.

I did not know why I wept all spring
Or what I longed for.

NAUSICAA

What am I looking for here anyway?
Why can't I stay away from the long panes
Giving on to an ordinary garden?
Again and again I walk up to the window and stare.
The steady yard leans into the rain, coloring.

Hyacinths stir in a bravery of daffodils
Clustered at the base of winter-blackened posts
That brace the glistening fence.
Birch bark silvers in front of forsythia sprays.
What is the name for youngness? *Nausicaa.*

Nausicaa. And an apple tree
Turns this way in back of the burned out house next door.
Not mine, not for my sake
These dripping petals, these leaves beautifully breaking
Beyond green verges to be mirrored in wet slate.

My stammering heart! The pearling rain
Of return, and we face each other in a garden
Taking the lightest breaths
Of our lives. Diffident. Likest a sapling. Brave.
We stand in the lost springtime of our selves

At once withheld and given. Nausicaa.
I travel. I keep looking. I have nothing.
It all happened a long time ago.

for Elaine Warner

7

NIGHTS IN AUGUST

These evening walks—eternal heat and haze
And draining color. Deepening maples lift
Their green fathoms of leaves, and dissolve. I drift,
Dissolving. Fences and houses dissolve. And days.

Nocturnal calm floats down, engulfing grays,
Drowning identity in the lightless rift
Of time. Summer nights vex obscurely. I shift,
Restless near sunset, until I fix my gaze

Where I find my peace—within. Then silence mounds
In immortal meadows, near an ocean bright
With cobalt of morning: the shores of early childhood.
There I discover house, dock, greenwood,
Rowboat—things and their names, as memory rounds
Each fact with its own past. I breathe that light.

BLUE GINGER: DÉJÀ VU

Deep as lapis, upon their green stems
Flower these glimmering flames of ginger.
Our gaze keeps swimming in,
Allured to the quiet place where blue lies pooled.
Dark leaves. Whorled dark flowers.
As if we were staring at candles,
We fall silent, turning to blue flowers.

How slowly they open into the glowing mind!
They shine doubled, as if already
Remembered. The shock of peace.
The shade of our lost lives burns into bloom
And returns to us, trembling with imminence.
What can we be sure of, lifted to the soft edge
Of vision? Only the blue fire,
Like ginger, blossoming.

for Harriet Gay

LETTER FROM SOUTH OF ROME

These nights—they are all the same.
I cannot forbear now. I write you these lines.
The summer has grown too old.
Too many hundreds of nights we have lived apart
Farther from each other in the same country
Than stars from Rome.
A difficult journey overland winter or summer
Many times delayed.
The sorrow this time is to us.
Your gifts do not any longer console me,
Not knife or lamp or jar, though I touch them. Silent.
Not even the silver talisman that has kept me safe.
Maybe the goblet you and I passed between us
When we drank the black wine.
The wine glints as I pour it under starlight.
I drink from the full glass
And find, staring from the base of the bowl
Where the stem is bonded,
A blue eye.

Starry night.
When for the darkness you can't read these words any longer,
Fold my letter into your coat.
Do not be afraid
To drink in the wastes of the northern provinces
As I do here
A wine so black it brings down the stars.

FOUR FISHING SONGS

Translated from the Hawaiian, *Pele and Hi'iaka*

1

Ha'a

A million fish!
Quick flashes in salt water
That dance as fast as my hands pounce
Dancing to grab them.

Ha'a, the bent-knee dance
Naked at full noon on the beach.
Ah, low down and close,
Near the water.

And the fish got away,
Clear out of my hands, danced away,
The catch got away—gone—
The catch danced away.

2

Manō

You're a cold eyed little fish, Manō,
Nudging me with your lazy kisses,
But we're swimming in deep water now,
And you're sliding in and out of the weeds of the sea
So smooth and speedy—stabbing. God! you're big!
You're a shark! I'm done for!

3

Aloha Kona

I loved the glimmering fish I caught
In the sultry night
At home in Kona
That sheathed us both in the glimmering.

The nights are chilly now, my lover gone.

That was the first time.
We had never done that before.
I loved it,
His love, sheathed in the peace of Kona,
Glimmering.

4

Honokohau

Hard rain stings Honokohau
And sorrow's wind rises
That breaks off and scatters the *awa* leaves
Over Honolua harbor.
And where the leaves fall
From that swelling sorrow,
They gentle the sea water.

Then she goes down to the edge of the beach
To dig out *opihi* shells with her strong fingers,
And to rub her palms over the hairy sea moss,
And to clasp her man, to scratch his back with her nails
To mark him her own at the edge of that serene sea—
The girl who was hurt by the handless suffering of love.

And she is dead now, that girl.

THE WORD IN THE WATER AT KA'ENA

1

Where have the voices gone that years ago
Gave us courage to trust,
Though the wind sickle the precipice
And birds scream in the wilderness of air?

Whatever in our lives brought us to this raked ledge
Can drive us into the black folds of water beneath us
Afraid, unless we can find once more the word
Which, under the massed weight of the elements, seems gone.

2

The sun fails.
Rayed with four hundred golden oars,
It pulls back
Till it leans on the ravenous blue of heaven,
And the ocean floods over its fire.
It sinks forward.
The sounds we are trying to hear are drowned.

3

Ka'ena: the sea.
Brine of origin stands in these pools
Burning in gold sunfall.
Bright rain has filled them
And what salt has spilled past clefts in coastal rock.

4

Ka'ena: the hooked wings of the cliff.
They tilt sheer to the stretch of stones and baking dirt
That scrape the bird's wild throat
Tasting of dust.
Against that gray reach of wings,

Banked black rock and red rock rise from the ocean naked
In an ignorant rim.

Bruised by the white waves of years,
They've grown stupid with long standing.
Reared in another age, they stay,
Counter to flight.
The cliff swerves above, pitching down through blue air
To the verge of the sea.
The surf pours forward,
And, under green walls of water, the rocks endure.

5

At Ka'ena in the night when the birds are still,
And their cries,
And the ocean at low tide pulls down the coastline
As if half asleep,
Sometimes there are strains like songs, voices
Praising the old ways,
Ghosts of those who ran forward to the other world
Exultant,
Chanting on the path as night avalanched behind them
Casting rocks.

They believed the wings of the great bird who brooded on the ocean
When the world began
Would bear them up: they would not become dust and nothing.
They plunged into death's unfathomable water
Trusting the mystery.
The power of their lives still tells us of them.

6

We are of our own age.
The names we give to things are not the same
As the names they gave.
We may not at first understand.
Yet the sea is as it was. The rocks have not changed.
By faith the living presences remain,
And, far beneath the forward-thundering surf
In the silence the world is founded on,
Abides alone the Everlasting Word.

ALONE AT AINAHOU: THE NEW LAND

I don't say your name anymore.
If at sunbreak I'm walking a road
Where ohia trees rise out of pasture grass—
So one with themselves they cannot turn
When wind strikes their ashy branches—
After a night rain has made shine
Bundles of baling wire and the fine spider lines between them,
And the stripped wood of logs for fencing;
When everything on the ranch brightens with water—
Stone, and the lichen on it, big hunks of lava,
The tanks, the pipes, the benches, the house, the outbuildings—
Everything all at once with water, I shiver,
The sun breaks,
But I do not turn.
I don't even say your name.

II

If the red fruit had been wind-fallen from the appletree, given to eat,
If we had not had to weep or suffer or leave Paradise, absent ourselves
From all that we loved best, would we not have come to Chartres anyhow?

CHARTRES

Saints in the old stone of the portals
Bless us.
Rain drizzles on slabs at the entrance.
Drops shape and fall down the iron staves of the fence.
When I touch the door, the wood is colder than dawn.

Inside, by tangible olive or lavender light,
I find in all the things men made in praise of Him
Why God so loved the world He forgave us.
The strong cathedral walls exhale our striving
Like a vapor, almost alive,
Like our own breath.

I'm alone here, very nearly.
December's rain keeps other travelers away.
But ghosts crowd Christ's airy altars
Through changes of raw light
Still telling their prayers.
They have no other place to stay.
I fall silent, listening to them.
Like them, I have no home, unless it is here.
The chill of fear. I shudder.
Saints
Intercede for me.
I kneel, barren before God.
My work is no fit gift. It fails.
Burning, I bear my fault,
And offer tears, graceless as I look up,
                                             lost
In the windows, stilled wheels
Turning light. How they jewel the pillars
And stir blue stain into glooms
Flooding these ancient wooden carvings—
All the great work of man given God

Lives saved in their labor
For centuries.
These ghosts are strong.

But has that been enough for them?
Even if our labor redeems us—
Us who for labor are cherished and changed—
Is that enough for a life?
O altitudes
                we walk among
                            out of our human love
I want to believe
                more
                        than I have
                                in my hands,
Ministers of light!

If the red fruit had been wind-fallen from the appletree, given to eat,
If we had not had to weep or suffer or leave Paradise, absent ourselves
From all that we loved best, would we not have come to Chartres anyhow?
I know that I am naked
                        and must labor
                                    and will die
Alone.
But I want back what grace once gave.
                            Still
                                    terrible God
Forgive me.

THE CHILL OF DISTANCE

Closed windows, heavy glass. Glass so thick
I can't hear the wind I see shake the stiff 'ohai,
The raintree's leafy shield.
I can't hear the racked eucalyptus wail
Or pelted bushes that brush the pane.

This is the way our world might seem to a god
Who is not with us—clear but soundless—
As if at once close and very far off.
Or to lovers who dream the face of the loved other,
The one they may never see again yet forever trust.

The chill of distance. A ghastly design of leaves
In back of glass. The streaming leaves,
The plunges they take in the dark,
Their rearing, their riding, their abrupt halts,
And all entirely silent, sealed by a frame.

Such beauty murders, strikes a blow there's no balm for,
A cold pain, the stone of a slow fright growing inside,
Or a livid bruise on the skin. As if I were dead,
Nothing that happens where you are seems real to me.
But I am not dead. I have no love left

And these heavy storms are like love,
These leaves, the breath of the wind going through them,
The rain flailing and tearing at them in the early dark,
Night coming down bare into the world.
The hardness of life without shelter.

But I have to go out there into the gale
Beyond the dense silence of the glass
Into the rain slapping on the other side,
And hear the leaves singing their panic aloud
As they fall in the frenzied wind. It is my life.

THE GHOSTS OF WHO WE WERE

On this humid December afternoon
Tall clusters of shell ginger, borne out of reach,
Hang over the sidewalk, quiet and undemanding as prayer.

But because you and I have separate lives now
In regions of the world far from one another
Who were once at peace here, resolved in our happiness,

Because we are divided by more than water
And land and climate, I think of winter in a place
Halfway between us, where our spirits are watching

As night comes on. These ghosts of who we were
Do not sleep. They wade in the high winds
Of a midcontinental blizzard, until they stand

Beyond the piled snowdrifts where they can see railtracks
Disappearing both directions, west and east.
Assured, they are as cold as trees.

They wait. Then the tracks begin to ring on the ties,
And, as the ties brace for the weight of many cars,
A bell clatters, and a wheeling light drives a bright beam

Far ahead through dense snowflakes. Then they grip hands,
The land shudders, the train wails by the crossing.
And they stare after it a long time, down the road they cannot go.

ICE FLOWERS

Shimmer of mist
Slurs the warm back of the mountain, and the mist vanishes
Like spray blown back from green waves
Breaking beachward in a brisk wind.
I can't believe it.
What I trust is cold—
Snow flowers with bracts of ice.

We stood in our boots on the sea wall by the bay.
Wintry water nudging the sand sank in.
Snowflakes laced the stinging air,
Crusted the brambles, slid off the shiny rose hips.
Ridged in ice, we held each other close,
Your mouth red, your breath warm, your face wet.
We stood there.

A frozen time.

We live apart
In a world not worth the saving.
The years advance.
Our lives like mist or sea spray vanish into them.
No crimson flowers wintering through absence
Gild the rising cold.

DECEMBER LIGHT

The sweet mountains drift in green haze.
June's on the way. The sun's deep in the ground.
Tilled acres are filled with warm seed.
Too soon.
I need the slow season so much now sometimes
I can feel on my body December's watery light.
How cold the glass was that the sun shone through
On you undoing the buttons slowly
So you could lay down your head on my breast
Before you left.

I grow pale as winter remembering how we took our time
(And the going so close)
As if we had the whole year for such candor,
And we had not.

All spring you've been gone.
The days grow long.
Still I could say it is all right for you to be slow
Coming home, if only you come.

But I can't.
The brief spring burns away
Our final season.
Soon we will rest forever motionless
Under a sun that holds no season for us.
Everything will be cold that touches us.
Even each other.

Then bring back winter again,
The sun on the zodiac
Halted at solstice,
Cold at the brink,
While we take our time with each other,
Close, under slow December light.

SUNSET

We didn't choose it.
The light, gathering slowly for hours
Above the long riverway,
Leaned over, at first growing paler,
And sang itself to us
Until we had to listen.

Then it compelled us to answer, to speak of it.
"Coral color," gentle on the underside of blue clouds fracturing.
"And rose," brightening as those broken clouds became darker.
"Is there a name for that redness beginning?"
"Garnet. Carmine. Fire."
"Yes. Yes. Those colors."

Then it took hold of us.
Wide layers of unshaken light crossed the west
Green-gilding the air, till its grave music
Undid us, and we fell silent.

For miles behind, it was already night.
Then around us, night, and night ahead of us.
At last we could no longer see each other.
The light had let go.

HOME

All we've laid by against the world's change
May not be enough to save us.
We can lose everything.

Frond-littered Haleiwa Beach
And the wide winter surf
That steepens over the reef pure cobalt,
Glassy aquamarine.

Small trees in the back yard in Jamestown
Safe from the wind,
Quince the color of coral, apricot that passes early,
And apple that scatters near the shielding wall
What blossoms it bears—
All their flowering branches, sweet, late fruit.

Houses where we've lived in Erie—
Lintels, floorboards, stairs,
Whose wood feels softened from our having walked there,
Glass doorknobs we've grasped—prisms breaking sunlight
Fallen through wavery panes into its many colors—
Furniture and rugs, window curtains,
Mirrors keeping our images in mind,
Rooms that hold our having talked in them,
Our having found each other.

All these bear the touch of our history,
And slowly our lives work toward the same home.

But we can lose everything we have: It can all be wasted.
We've lived everywhere,
But then there will be no place on earth for us.

RAINWATER

The shades are pulled, but still I hear the rain. Under the streetlight
The street glistens in my mind, burnished in the same rainwater
That has been coming back

Since the first cloud-cover drenched the first burning stone of the world.
The same rain, its common shining. But this night is singular.
I want to hold it.

Yet it is not this night but you I want to keep, miracle
In the century of my own life, safe to the centuries after,
Just as you are—

The very gesture of your hands pushing back through your white hair,
Or your teeth biting your underlip as you dance, your eyes held
On an inward vision,

Like the chosen of God, who dance where the Rock of Origin remembers
The earliest rains. Yet what can they know as it was from long vanished history?
There's only rainwater.

The human part of those ancient faiths which still live in our own time,
Once real as the beautiful names of Israel, is lost sight of,
Is general as the rain.

Even for my own need I can't find words to carry you clear of this age,
Yet known as yourself. We live only in time, and what is historical passes,
Leaving relics.

And even the relics of history pass. But the rain comes back always the same.
When you have left me, I will imagine you sometimes, but only rainwater
Will be as I imagine.

SONNET: THE HIDDEN CHRYSOPRASE

These years are winter. The skies are overcast with dramatic clouds. When they break heavily, as they will, all around us the snows will begin. Fallen too wet for the slopes to hold, they will fall underneath, loosening an avalanche of rubble upon too frail and kind a thing to live in such cold.

This is possible.

These years are winter. The stars on glassy nights still wheel in the old constellations according to law, abiding the brink, the space, the vacant abyss. Turning under and rising away from horizons, going from us and coming back forever to us, starfalls are the hidden promises we hold.

This also is possible.

These years are winter. Cereus, night-blooming, in a warm house, has one flower to be borne. Cactus, the crooking stems keep safe the nectar in their flesh. Their spines are cruel. We do not know the time when we will open the door of a room upon a strange glow of apple-green chalcedony, chrysoprase, in whose white blossom deeply cupped is held the pollen all these years have gathered.

And this is possible.

Or they are nothing.

AFTERNOON

I don't know anyone anymore. It's late.
We have been driving a long while
And, but for infrequent cars and vans
Passing down soft highway lanes,
Nothing has moved for miles.
Over slopes opening on either side of the turnpike,
Autumnal yellow has evened out meadow and sky.
Everything we see is the same.
Dry light seeps into dust and remains dry.
What has become of your children?
Though the sere trees have waned,
We have not yet seen any leaves fall.
They hang still.
I thought of wind,
But the yellow lakes doze, placid as a coat of paint.
Naturally the fences are not shaken.
We should get out.
We need more than ourselves.
I can't remember your sister's name.
Usually there are many blue flowers this time of year—
Roadside asters. We have not seen any.
All the sumac has turned tawny colored.
Yellow. Null sunlit yellow. Yellow.
Nothing will ever change.

THE CITY IS AN ISLAND

The month is warm October.
Out of green bags ripe rubbish unfolds upon the boulevards.
Plague is blackening where the sun is spreading
In a flat intense film on the walls of the capitol.
No chips of light glitter from bright granite.
The glare in the neighborhoods, too level and too heavy,
Oppresses new automobiles and red hedge flowers.
Refuse blows about the beaches
In a dirty wind. Papers slide a little.
The slack sea slaps upward into trash
That no one takes care of:
There is not land enough.

For the city is an island.
It has always been an island.

And it is sealed.
A city should shudder and warp
With contradictory noises
After early traffic subsides.
Here instead is an undifferentiated humming
With dead intervals
Into which bird cries fall without ringing.
Everywhere silence increases
Because voices sound wrong.

And you live here.
You have wished for a bridge,
And there are no bridges.
Elsewhere you've seen the steel spans
Arching from concrete
That lift dark roads and hang them over a bay.
But this island lies where it will never be joined.
Nothing is close enough.
It is alone.

It can fail of its own folly.
That failure can defeat you.
But you cannot walk away,
Raise a rebuffing hand,
Give up and go home:
This is where you live.

Daily the jets depart in their single gesture,
The splendid arc of escape.
Their freedom is not yours.
You live here.
The island is your city.

You live where what is human has gone wrong.
For this the red earth reeks, the ocean is foul,
The filming air corrosive.
The island chokes.

How will you save it?

You will have to swallow the unconditional promise
Given you years ago of kindness exchanged.
It will not hold; its taste is tears and ashes.

You have to embrace another passionate image
As old as forgiveness. Grow strong, labor,
And bid to the mind's eye a savage friend and a cold
Who loved the law and kept it with wisdom and simpleness,
And measure by that image how much you honor the city.
You will not even want to leave.

again, for Jean King

CLEFT OF LIGHT

Fallen among heavy wind-blown grasses greening the ridge,
Daylong we lay glistening, hidden in sun, mingling kisses,
And something essential left us, cleft and entered the hill and rested,
To stay forever secret there among the weeds.

All things change. The air goes dead by noon. Discolored sun
Leaches the ridge. Dust in the vale of rocks twists and rises.
Night comes down. A small moon lifts above two cloven figures
Fast in stone, narrowly dividing them with light.

RODOLPHO: A LATER WINTER

Amber of last light reddens.
Stony December has frosted the leaded glass.
The library fire is out. He kneels to light it.
The paper flares and catches.

                      Mimi.

Burning through every hour of his life
To a blaze that froze in Paris decades before.
Longer.
A knock at the door. Mimi.
Your hands were icy. You warmed them near my stove
By flames as frail against the bitter weather
As your shawl.
You shivered in my arms at the slanted skylight.
The hard moon bore down blue on the wooden floor.

In my heart the snow begins.
Briefly, touched by belief, we stood at the window
Looking down over the city, the lamps coming on.
I was ignorant then of how strong roofs had to be
To lift those masses of night away from the street.

When you dropped the key to your door, I blew out the lamp.
I didn't want you to find it.
Chill metal. It's somewhere in my desk.

Festival memories ribbon through the mind
Confusing frost and music, pranking the square
With taffeta sleeves—showy green, crimson, gold—
Lifting to all of us tea-colored brandy in glasses
As cold as coins, and still upon the stars
Ringing
The unfading song of your name.

                      Mimi.

Happiness has no force. It was midwinter.
The ground was hard, the bright air ached with ice,

And even the daze and glister of snowflakes falling—
The gentlest gesture heaven gives, I think—
Felt cruel: there was nowhere to go to keep warm.
We were shut out
By spiked iron gates and a wall of granite blocks.

Whatever I have or love came after that
And was changed because of you.
And you—your fire had gone out, your hands were cold.

for Richard Gullicksen

THE COLD

The earth is acrid with smoke. Cracked bronze leaves
Rattle into the wind. Clouds, scattered past
The creaking oaks, begin to lapse into scarves
Of russet on skeletal figures. Goodbye. The last
Utterance. Take my hand one time. So.
Nothing in my life has made me ready for cold
Like this—a blast from the chasm. Look there—a crow
Is flapping down dusk. Gone now. Flown into gold.

Nothing we say can matter anymore.
Nothing we do can alter what we've done.
These words that fall are nothing. What are they for,
When bird, leaf, bonfire, cloud are gone?

Ourselves. They are the seal that was made to hold.
I loved you. But nothing is safe from the cold.

III

The sovereign happiness
Whose abiding place
Is now here among us
In the flower of beautiful bodies and beautiful souls. . . .

Castiglione, *The Courtier,* Book IV

IN URBINO

I

In cold Urbino love is spoken of
Still in the old tongue. Our changed lives bear witness.
We know what we could not have known
Before we climbed the steep streets to the palace
To stand at the same window where the Duchess
Stood gazing, on that last "fair morning
The color of roses."
To our very great sadness,
Since it is lost—
Urbino is lost to us
As we are to each other.
No city but this could repay the long drive uphill
In winter, the night arrival at the hour
When all the doors were locked which later stood open.

I have to speak of it because of what happened there
And praise it all my life.

II

We stayed for a time in Venice. There
A silvery sense of water licking porches
Slipped about our ears with a touch as light as breath,
And the stone gave way to the Adriatic Sea
As it always had. One evening, walking late,
When sun dumped gold into the Grand Canal,
Our hands tightened, as if we gripped big jewels
Against the dying light.

Did I startle you? I gave way with a sigh
The long withholding.
You said, "I have something for you,"
And pulled from your coat a broken figure
Made of red clay. "See how the body gleams

And gathers light."
The darkness rustled.
There was a scent of almonds.
Your fingers glanced my breast
Clumsily. I gasped. You
Caught me close
And held me, trembling.
Tentative at first, we came to trust
Even the most common gestures of our hands.

Though Venice's splendid spires and palaces
Could never be home for us,
I came upon morning
There: A tree. Five oranges glowing
From the green of the glossy leaves lifting out of the vapor
Which rose off the white canals.

Now, as Venice blooms in my mind, all its fixed images
Pulse through an apricot haze,
And shafts of washed gold burn and slide together,
Ubiquitous around the swimming buildings.
Again I hear rich cries, like call notes of birds
Waking. I listen; the cries subside, falling,
And are taken back into the ancient silence,
Where they cannot be cancelled, though we never go back to Venice.

III

We traveled the worn-out coastal plain too long
And were late finding the road that rose to Urbino
Through the bony Appenines. As night lowered,
Pooling soft knots of houses on the slopes
In lapis lazuli, we fell silent.
I was thinking of Castiglione and of Yeats
Who came this way—

The wind blowing their voices in the air
That crossed our maps.
                                        At the summit,
Nothing but darkness overhead, and winter falling
Upon the town, as we drove inside the walls.

IV

How can we speak of love when all we have
Is the silence that broadens between us?
Involuntary syllables break from us,
And the silence closes around them again, forever.
Yet I don't think given love diminishes
When it changes this way.
It is red earth, ground for our lives,
Air, fire, and water—what Urbino's courtiers
Believed everything issued from.

V

In Urbino the old words rose in our breath again
The same as in the four-night conversation
They rose and rang in Guidobaldo's palace
More than four hundred years ago.
We praised the world, its comeliness and order,
And man, its mirror, the great wheel of stars
And seasons, sun and moon, the courtly ways
Of government, of virtue, and of learning.
But chiefly love.

Love was the stony street we climbed,
The high window we looked from, smiling
After the tireless talk, love was the hill
Of the city, love, the walls, the weather, the clearness
Of morning air, the mountain-wandering wind.
Love was all that we were, a thousand times over

Forgiven and trusted, love, the hail
That rakes the naked outcrop,
Love, the cry of a man who has chosen wrong
At last and forever and knows it.

VI

Castiglione said he bore from those years,
To him the happiest four, sorrow's crown
Because they were gone. "What cannot be rehearsed
Without tears, there is a wilderness of sorrow
In that death, whose grief passes all the others,
Though all are dead,
So far that excellence surpassed the rest."

VII

I carry one fact through all the years remaining:
Beside the mountain road downward to Florence
Four houses stand, of stone, and bare as truth,
Blurred, in rainclouds, hyacinthine sky.

Buildings are monuments.
They mark the places words as pure as fire
Rang in before they sank into the ground
Which keeps them.

VIII

For a brief time we were changed to angels
And beheld "the sovereign happiness
Whose abiding place
Is now here among us
In the flower of beautiful bodies and beautiful souls."
Once and once only and never again.
Further than that, love cannot be disclosed.

GHOSTS

It is dusk in the small room.
Snow shrills upon stiff panes.
The radiator hisses beneath the sill.
The gloom inhabiting the four corners
Feels out the rug, the bookshelves,
The surface of the oak desk,
The deep armchair,
The sweaters folded there.
Slowly our eyes take in what is here
Then come to each other.
Our fingers are quiet,
Our bodies are slack and attentive,
As if we were listening for someone breathing,
For a word breaking, for whatever comes—
That still.

Then the street lamp comes on . . .
A frame of yellow light upon the floor,
And the room goes dark.
But something strong is with us.
We will never leave this house.

WHAT PASSED

Both of us were shy
Of the promise
By the early grave
Of the child whom
The rain-spending fall gave,
So young she died,
So late comes happiness,
So much in solitude.
David.
We have no home but this
Rainy low hillside,
Nor will we ever have,
Unless we receive
What we crave
When we grieve
For it—not years after.

for John David Walker

NO ONE

In Albany or Norfolk or any city at all,
You catch the tang of yellow ginger—air
Suddenly sweet with it, and you turn to it. Where
Does it come from? But there is nothing there. It's gone,
Phantom. No damp, living flowers. No one.

Or when a white fog surrounds you, where you walk
By a barberry hedge, near the railroad in Kingston or Newark,
You hear a known voice beside you say your name,
A friend's, and you answer, yes, yes? The same
Thing: An apparition. A thought. No one.

But the voice, sibylline, the vanishing scent—so close!
Gone. *The light wind fell and said nothing. The house
Kept its own counsel. The grass looked on but held still.
They were there when you bore the grief which broke your life.
They go everywhere with you now. They always will.*

A GUST OF WINTER

In the last hour of this ordinary day
The blue ginger flowers by the pool
Cease shaking and grow quiet, as they color with rain.
It is an old garden. The years have been slow
That gave these green cypresses time to be tall
Over a stone bench hidden by lilies.

I have one daughter and three sons, whose lives are my solace.
Their kindnesses scatter around me
Like the small leaves tossing away from the raintree.
Their beauty deepens as these tropic days do
Around the pool. I can leave them now,
Trusting their happiness enough.

What is this shivering? Presage? Or ghosts
Crossing? Or a gust of winter?
But winter will never come this far south.
Winter will not come, nor love by cold light
Wrestled from ice and hardened in the North Wind,
The sky ringing like struck rock.

To live without winter: Who lives here has to learn how.
To be daily at peace in the sun,
Or else, since there's no coming back, leave the garden forever
To hazard the crystalline reaches where there is no haven
In the stony air from blizzards, sheer lakes, white cataracts,
Or the amorous knives of the snow.

I'll stay no longer with ghosts in their green garden
But go where winter-beaten flakes out of blind heaven
Obscure the nightfall, the more gently for the strange cold.
There's such kindness in the snow's gestures, and such need for it
In the wind that sweeps the wastes far from here—
Winter's unsparing country.

for Maxine and Earll Kingston

ON THE LEDGE

Strange how yesterday's afternoon light
Fell wan off the studio walls.
I had thought they'd seem brighter, more solid.

My friend's plain kindness.

When I couldn't sleep last night,
I got up around four
And put my fingers on the stone sill
To watch dark snow filling ledges
That had glistened all summer with heat.
I stood there a long time.

What can I give in return?

I will not cover my face
Against the dawn's cold breaking.

for Ben Norris

49

BLUE FLOWERS

1

All January, cold had gouged the ground
Under the rigid highways. Ploughs worked nights
Pushing snow out of the roads. For weeks it mounted
Alongside city traffic. Though the sun
Blazed before nightfall, crimson, green, and gold,
Slanting through blue ice, nobody noticed.
Withdrawn far into their frozen lives,
People walked fast, keeping their eyes down,
Pulling their thick coats closer.

2

It is late afternoon.
In a cafe near the airport turnoff, a man and a woman
Sit at a formica table over their supper.
They gaze and gaze on each other's shining face.
Both are smiling. Their eyes are wet,
Their tears the bright gage of a given word
Which lifts from them now,
Strong as the crystalline blue above the city,
Wide-reaching as the winterfast countryside.

3

What sweet wind, of spring or winter,
Carries our promises,
And where does it take them
When we who gave them are gone?

4

They abide. Chance can confound us or time
Slip the knots of our strength. We fail.
But the covenants witness
That we become saints when we dare to take on a promise,
Its weight and fortune, speaking words which we cast
In the teeth of what must be. They hallow the air
They are made of, and make safe the place where they stay,
Whatever heaviness or danger
Come to their makers afterwards because of them.

5

This oath I swore in another century:
"I have always known you. All my life I will love you.
When I die, I will come to you. Never again will I leave."

6

The summer winds have swept the land with loosestrife,
Lavender, gentian, vetch, vervain, wild aster.
Faith was their seed, their field—unbroken silence.
They grew from the lasting covenants we made.
Now thousands of acres avalanche with blue,
Such force our promises have to come to flower.

BY WHOSE AUTHORITY?

I Who are you?

> At first I am only breath in a bright room.
> Always at first I am afraid, gone stiff and tender.
> The wings crowd my throat,
> And my fingers pluck and flutter at webs
> In front of eyes looking for what I am
> Hiding
> A thing so simple
> That I am ashamed for its sake that my body carries it
> And that it is sacred.
>
> That it is sacred.
>
> Remembering that,
> There rises in me a night, a lake, a silence
> My body can move in
> Finding the other.
>
> You are the other,
> Known to me from the first time I took breath
> From inward light
> Finding other forms for who you are.

II What is your family?

Light as leaves, the only name I have,
No other given to hold me
Down, a stone safe against wind or water
Or a sound to let go in the breath-shape of a ghost

I've tried to find my name.
Holding quiet, I've heard the air talk
And the upland earth and the long sands.
I've learned how to listen inside
Cliff rock, beach rock, hill stone, shore stone, sure of
What screams in a raw wind turned on a point, knowing
What drones in the surf and drowns human voices
But I do not know how to call my family here
Or even who they are.
Stranger.

What leaves, leaves
The breath of the land runs through
And weaves in a voice
With the white words of a stranger

Without any name of power
What can I give?
What word-spell can I weave?

The wind comes back.
The steady sound of the sea grows less than it was.

I give what I have.
Breath in the leaves becomes a song.

III Who is your teacher?

No one. Earth.
Dust. Stone. Dry midsummer's rubble.
When I was a child
Hunkered one day in warm dust to watch ants
About their work,
As if remembering a dead life,
I knew I was myself the dust they lived in
And that they were the seeds of my death.

I know the will of my ribs and my skull to be earth again.

No one. Air.
The mounting heaven of day
That battens on promise and gathers prayer
And pours back radiant answers from bright cloudbanks.
And the deep heaven of night—atmosphere of the mind.
I used to reach my hands out over the sill.
A responding spirit filled them with flakes from stars.

I trust the lifting of breath to ask. Something spills back.

No one. Water.
Sounding or still.
I was a sullen child
Pitched into thought by the cold
Rankling my heart
Until I gave way at last at the edge of the sea,
My silence balanced against that massive water.
The ocean flogged her breakers, glint and sparkle
Rinsing and rinsing the shale
And raveling back,
One icy silver—water, earth, and sky—
That fell everywhere and hung falling everywhere,

Pulse of all things living solved to one,
And I was one.

I live by raveling water everywhere.

No one. Fire.

A sweet flame flickering runs beneath my skin.
Pale as I am, I color, rosy with love.
My limbs tremble. The bravest thing
Would be to raise my eyes and face his eyes.
I am near to fainting. Parched. Suffused with fire.

There is likeness, but that fire does not seem the same

As the thundering flames that poured in waves
Breaking around the attic and the upstairs rooms
Of the great house on North Avenue.
Red ravened, brighter than blood against the moon.
Crimson behind the blackened window frames
Roared like a wind.
I could see the heavy curtains afire
And the bed, the table beside it, the iron lamp
Standing in fire, all rising consumed,
Flaring into the darkness
Under fiercely played hoses.
Old Isaac lived there.
I was the child he led up charred stairs
In the morning to scorched books,
The wet wood reeking of smoke.

Over the dead house at night, the stars swung,
Burning.

There is fire from Heaven not like that conflagration,
The page quiet underneath the hand,

And in the mind, flames wavering around dreams, consuming them—
The synapse, the distance bridged, the closing.

It is the same fire.
Fire is my teacher.

KAILUA BEACH

1

If you are not here, I cannot touch you.
Then what shall I do under the sun with my body?
Drowse. Sprawl face down on the glittering beach,
Fiddle sand through my fingers. But not think of you.

2

Not think. Eyes tighten on the wrinkling glare
Of water that fractures miles along the shoreline.
I think of miles. The same light does not fall
Here as falls where you are. I pour moon's
Equal silver over mind's Carolina
Where you will fall asleep. I think to breathe
In the temperate air where office, hospital, house
Rest, dream-washed by imperturbable blue.
I think to take to my body some of the patience
Buildings have at night. That cold color.

3

Only I don't. I image an abstract room.
Summer outside. Shine of a silver window.
You, asleep in white sheets. I touch them. Warm.
My fingers. Your face. Your hair bristling. And I tremble.
Ah, but it's sand in my fingers, at my cheek, harsh,
Under my breasts, and sun tense at my back.

4

Kailua Beach—a shore slung around a bay,
Casually beautiful, as if it had been imagined
Easily, and in an offhand gesture
Made tangible. Before we touched each other
I came here sometimes, dreaming we might meet

And speak in this common light. But the day I saw you,
I was so shaken by fright I covered my face.

5

I would not now. Love in love's substance lives.
You have become so familiar to my hands
That almost by thinking I touch you, I can touch you.
But there's only the gradual surf and the sand. And a shudder
Of running steps. My heart suddenly winces
In my ribs, strikes, as I turn to face what seems
Almost your frame, close, improbably haloed.

6

Not you. I breathe. But I think in some sense you
Are alive in me as I brush off grains of sand
Stuck to my skin. My flesh. My flesh is breath
Catching on images, thought-nicked. A salty taste.
A smell of beach and sweat. A vision of light
Brilliantly cast in cerulean water, and of islands
Offshore that darken or shine as the sun sweeps them,
Of the wave's fall and return down the curved littoral.

7

Ah, I do wish you were here with me,
So in your hands I live. But I've had enough
Of the moony Carolina fantasy makes
In the racket of truth. Sometime maybe the moon
Will scatter silver over us there. Or maybe
Not. Fact is the loveliest world there is:
Kailua Beach: The always spangled sea
And there, high up, five crank-winged frigate birds,
Rapt in their flight, are coasting the fabulous azure.

8

How lively the ocean glistens, its keen salt
Stinging and flecking my arms. The water slides
Around me, heaving blue breakers ashore. I hear
The sound of their fall and the water-tingle in my ears
As I turn and dive under a swell, while my body
Rises, drifts, thinks, thinks water, blue water
Rising and falling, sun, hot glitter of air,
Salt water falling and falling, holding my body,
Bearing me safe and easy in the bay.

HEALERS

1

Fire at her back,
A flaming coronal, hair, black
Midnight, pitch,
Rivery, pointed with light, rich
As a warm rose
In the cold dusk of departure, or the close
Of a music, smiling,
Her mind at play, owl-eyed, beguiling
As the Sibyl, secret,
Sweet in the smoke of a pink cigarette.

2

Still as a glass, I listen for the sound
The Sun makes burning into Earth the wheeling
Seasons. Out of the roar one hour will ride
A wind: Again I stand at a window, bound
On a rack of moonlight. Eyes fixed on the ceiling,
My lost love lies in bed. The while, outside,

As long as the wind soughs in the wailing pines,
A glory storms through rocking silver light.
He leaves, and then there gather, slowly reeling
Around me, mantic fires. Unlit, they shine
With the calm of hours to come, the fury of night
Gone. And all that stays is the gift: Healing.

WHAT WE LEARNED

We have a history now,
Rich with account and act,
As long as a Congress or a war,
As worn with poverty and hope as any nation,
Or as our lives before we met.
None of this was miracle.

The sea does not need our sacrifices.
Rain is not God's thought for us.
Stars are not holes shot through a stone canopy into sacred light.
Winter can turn to summer without our prayer
And fall to winter as before.

If I embrace you, you will weep.
If you leave me, I will endure.
There are reasons. We have learned what they are.
A miraculous change would have taught us nothing
But praise.

HERMIONE

Almost winter again. The trees are bare.
The finally quiet lake
Brims with reflected evening. Only the air
Shivers, about to break
With snow. As I give way to the cold, I find
What it is the years have yielded, hold it in mind,

Then release it into the dusk. The clear water,
Glassing the gathered sky,
Hides dark lives. They have pulled the sun through the mirror
And changed, as a wracked cry
Held back can change to a song. And now, silence.
Yet something is unfolding there—a presence

A quavering glitter, beams, radiated
From the core of a drowned star.
Faint at first, a fire catches. I've waited
Enough. The time that was far,
Whose coming I trusted, is close as the last gold spill
Of sun at the edge of the lake. I've but to be still—

It will come. Faith—it has nothing to do with promise.
I have known the strongest vow
To fail. But not faith fail. The very grass
That lives through winter now
Lies hidden: All that was freely loved and let go
Returns, of its own strong will, after the snow.

for Bacil

POETRY FROM ILLINOIS

History Is Your Own Heartbeat
Michael S. Harper (1971)

The Foreclosure
Richard Emil Braun (1972)

The Scrawny Sonnets and
Other Narratives
Robert Bagg (1973)

The Creation Frame
Phyllis Thompson (1973)

To All Appearances: Poems New
and Selected
Josephine Miles (1974)

Nightmare Begins Responsibility
Michael S. Harper (1975)

The Black Hawk Songs
Michael Borich (1975)

The Wichita Poems
Michael Van Walleghen (1975)

Cumberland Station
Dave Smith (1977)

Tracking
Virginia R. Terris (1977)

Poems of the Two Worlds
Frederick Morgan (1977)

Images of Kin: New and
Selected Poems
Michael S. Harper (1977)

On Earth as It Is
Dan Masterson (1978)

Riversongs
Michael Anania (1978)

Goshawk, Antelope
Dave Smith (1979)

Death Mother and Other Poems
Frederick Morgan (1979)

Local Men
James Whitehead (1979)

Coming to Terms
Josephine Miles (1979)

Searching the Drowned Man
Sydney Lea (1980)

With Akhmatova at the Black Gates
Stephen Berg (1981)

More Trouble with the Obvious
Michael Van Walleghen (1981)

Dream Flights
Dave Smith (1981)

The American Book of the Dead
Jim Barnes (1982)

Northbook
Frederick Morgan (1982)

The Floating Candles
Sydney Lea (1982)

Collected Poems, 1930–83
Josephine Miles (1983)

The River Painter
Emily Grosholz (1984)

The Passion of the
Right-Angled Man
T. R. Hummer (1984)

Healing Song for the Inner Ear
Michael S. Harper (1984)

Dear John, Dear Coltrane
Michael S. Harper (1985)

Poems from the Sangamon
John Knoepfle (1985)

Eroding Witness
Nathaniel Mackey (1985)
National Poetry Series

The Ghosts of Who We Were
Phyllis Thompson (1986)

In It
Stephen Berg (1986)

46   186